Network Marketing Online

How To Recruit 1,042 Members In 6 Months Without Picking Up The Phone

by Eric Welke

Network Marketing Online: How To Recruit 1,042 MLM Members In 6 Months Without Picking Up The Phone

By Eric Welke

Eric Welke, Checkmate Marketing Group LLC

Legal Stuff

Table of Contents

About The Author 9

Introduction 11

Part 1: Laying Your Foundation... 13
How to Find the Best Network Marketing Business for You.............. 15
What to Expect When Joining an MLM Online Business..................... 18
Growing Your New MLM Business... 21
Recruiting Network Marketing Affiliates.. 24
Overcoming MLM Prospects' Reluctance 27
5 Avoidable Home Business Mistakes.. 30
Top Earner MLM Tips 34

Part 2: Succeeding Online 37
Finding MLM Resources Online 39
Online MLM Business Software Tools You Need to Master 43
Top 3 Sources of Targeted Traffic for Your Home Business............... 47

Part 3: Social Media Marketing.. 51
List of Social Networks for Sharing Your Content.............................. 53
Effective Social Network Page Management for Home Business 57
Strategies for MLM Online Marketing on Twitter............................... 63
How to get Facebook Fans on a Tight Budget 67

Part 4: Email Marketing 71
HTML Email Newsletters: What You Need To Know........................... 73
Tips for Writing an Effective Email Subject Line................................. 77
Improve Your Online Earnings Using Solo Ads 81

Part 5: Putting It All Together 85
Your Network Marketing Online Business Plan 87

Bonus Chapters 97
Sustaining Enthusiasm For Your Online Business.............................. 99
Thinking of Putting your Home Business on Auto-Pilot? 102

Epilogue 107

We Want Your Feedback on This Book!... 109

About The Author

Eric Welke is a 10 year internet and network marketing veteran. He went fulltime in this industry after being laid off from his corporate job and has never looked back. You can learn more about him by visiting his personal blog at **EricWelke.com**

Go to **http://ericwelke.com/readerbonus** to download the secret bonus exclusively for readers.

Introduction

Welcome to Network Marketing Online!

The multilevel marketing industry has been revolutionized over the past decade. No longer are networkers forced to spend endless hours in hotel meetings watching rehashed presentations, feebly hoping that the few people they were able to contact actually show up.

The internet, and especially social media, has extended the reach of multilevel marketing pros around the globe. Untold fortunes await those that understand how to grow their business through network marketing online.

This book will provide you with the knowledge you need to tap into this vast gateway to multilevel marketing success. It provides you the easiest and fastest way to get started with MLM recruiting and prospecting online today.

Whether you are into network marketing for beginners or are already a network marketing pro, you will find value here.

From The Author: "Network Marketing Online is filled with the strategies, tactics and resources I use everyday to achieve network marketing success. What you will learn here has enabled me to recruit 1,042 members in only 6 month – all without chasing down friends and family, going to hotel meetings, listening to boring presentations or cold calling leads.

I was recently named as the top producer in one of the MLM companies I work with. It is my hope that you can experience results like this with the help of this book and become a network marketing pro."

Part 1: Laying Your Foundation

Even in the age of the internet, there are some things in network marketing that will never change. This first section goes over some of the basics you must do to ensure you have the right business, the right product, the right team and the right setup for YOU. Of course we will apply this to a sustainable online business, rather than a traditional go and hunt people down at the mall "business".

How to Find the Best Network Marketing Business for You

If you want to try your luck with network marketing companies, there are many of them you can choose from. Finding out which is best for you will require some due diligence on your part. There are however, a few useful basic criteria you can use to find out which one is the best for you.

Keep in mind that knowing how to find the best network marketing business will also help you market the opportunity to other people. It's not enough to market a business opportunity based on the potential income. You need to be upfront with people about it and tell them what level of commitment is needed.

Cost of Entry

How much are you willing to shell out? One advantage of network marketing businesses is the lower cost of entry compared to traditional businesses. Although there are some companies that sell products at a premium price, you'll need to make sure that you can sell your product in the market it was made for. You'll have a hard time moving expensive supplements if the people in your area don't have the money for it.

This is the advantage of some lower priced network marketing products. It's easier to get new and repeat customers if the cash outlay is low. Compare a $40 a month expense versus a $10 subscription.

Your Level of Sales Experience

It's always a good thing not to bite off more than you can chew. Remember that a product is usually designed with a specific market in mind. If you're not familiar with selling to that particular market, it may not be a good idea to get into a business that caters to it. This downside can be mitigated if you have excellent training and support from your sponsor or upline.

Product's Growth Potential

Is there a need for the product? Is it a fad or does it have long term use?

It better be long term because the end game for network marketers is building a consistent residual income. You can't get residual income if the company won't last more than a few months after the fad has died.

Your Sponsor's Level of Support

More than anything, this influences how far a rookie network marketer can go. Getting the full support of your upline means you gain access to their experience and tools. You should take advantage of this.

On the other hand, if the person recruiting you isn't known for providing support to his team, then you're better off not joining. You can still join the same network marketing opportunity, if you can find a supportive team and sponsor.

Payout Schedule

It generally takes a few weeks or months before payout starts to come in regularly. Don't expect to earn immediately as there are usually quotas and targets that you need to meet before being paid.

When you study the payout program, try to gauge how long before you can get any stable income from your sales. It's critical info especially for those who want to go into marketing full time. You can't sell if you don't have the resources you need to run your campaign.

What to Expect When Joining an MLM Online Business

MLM Online Business is one of the most popular business models online. A lot of people are attracted to the prospect of building up a network that can eventually provide them with a decent passive income. There is also a lower cost of entry because you're re-selling what the MLM company is selling.

Veteran network marketers don't even stop at just one company. They join multiple networking businesses online and offer different products to their network. This is great if you have a large established network that can absorb multiple product offers.

It's a challenging and sometimes frustrating career choice where only the most determined last. Don't expect to get anywhere if you're not totally committed to marketing and building your network. And even if you do get a steady stream of sales, you still have to provide support for your recruit's recruits so they benefit from the business and become more productive.

If you've just signed up or if you're interested in joining an MLM Online Business, here are a couple of things to expect:

-        Not everyone wants to discuss network marketing as more than a few people have tried it out and failed. As much as possible, always use an honest approach that focuses on the benefits and giving details of what to expect. Hard sell tactics won't help you build a lasting network.

-      Network marketers and MLM companies have gotten a bad rap because of people who used the model to cheat their customers. If the payout is very generous and depends more on recruitment rather than moving product to consumers, then you might be joining the wrong company.

-      There is huge potential to gain a significant steady income but it cannot be done overnight. Don't ever use the "get-rich-quick" or similar approach as it is deceiving and not what network marketing is really about. Network marketing and MLM's end goal is to help people out to build their own business or passive source of income.

-      Popular niches, health & fitness for example, can be extremely competitive. Always try to find a niche that has a lot of potential customers but not too many competitors. Research is crucial.

-      Not everyone in your network will succeed, but you have a direct influence on his or her chances for success.

-      You will encounter people with different background, skills and levels of motivation. As their sponsor/upline/recruiter you should ensure that your team gets your full support.

-      Your success hinges a lot on your team. You have to make sure they're motivated and determined to reach their goal as much as you are.

-      For Online MLM some things become relatively easier like lead generation. There are a variety of acceptable ways that can be used to get contact information.

-      You should also allot enough time for your network. Looking for new leads is as important as building and maintaining your team.

-      Not all MLM online businesses are guaranteed success, so it's best to have several MLM offers carried on your network. You should be able to move to better performing products as needed.

Growing Your New MLM Business

Sustaining the growth of your new MLM business can be an uphill battle. This is true for both veteran and new entrepreneurs. The products being marketed maybe different but there are several challenges common to all.

Here are some of the most common challenges you may encounter with your new MLM business.

Slow Growth – this is a common complaint, but it is more an indicator of deeper issues. There are many factors that affect the growth rate of any online business. For new MLM business the most important is the rate of new people joining up. Since there are several possible causes of this issue, you'll need to go through some in-depth root cause analysis to find out what you need to do to fix it.

Inexperienced Marketers – It can be difficult for someone who has no selling experience to close a deal. Inexperience is a liability and can cause even a very interested lead to get turned off. You have to provide mentorship and coaching support for those team members who do not have marketing experience.

Low quality recruits – The quality of your recruits depend on both their motivation and marketing skill. You want to get some who has high marks on both, aside from the reliability and integrity you should come to expect.

Decline in Team Morale – There are several different factors that can cause this, but it can be minimized somewhat by effective and consistent communication. When you're growing a new MLM business you should expect to encounter challenges along the way and your team should be ready for it too. Effectively relaying news, whether good or bad, is an important skill to master.

Incorrect Setting of Expectations – Even if communication is done consistently, there is still a possibility that people will misunderstand the message. In the case of network marketing, there are some marketers who tend to sugarcoat offers to the point of over promising. This is a potential problem when people join the group with the wrong expectations. It can affect your own credibility, so you need to make sure that everyone in your team is on the same page.

New Product Introduction – Sometimes the main company that distributes the product will introduce something new. This can cause some disorientation at the start. At worst the new product will compete directly with the current product but it can also become an additional source of income for the team.

Root cause analysis is a very important tool in any team's arsenal. It will help you isolate the causes of each problem that you encounter. The trick is to exhaust all possibilities and data you can gather. Once you've identified the root cause then you can apply the correct fix.

Try to read other veteran marketers' experience when they started on their new MLM business. They usually have useful information on their blogs or Facebook pages. As most MLM business problems are similar in nature, you'll probably get a good starting to point for fixing your own.

Recruiting Network Marketing Affiliates

Let's face it, to get ahead in networking marketing you'll need to establish a solid team of productive affiliates. Recruiting network marketing affiliates is a critical task for any marketer. You'll need to look far and wide for these special individuals who are driven to succeed as much as you are. They aren't easy to find though and you'll need to cast as wide a net as possible to find the best candidates.

Your marketing team members may start out as one of your customers. After successfully closing a sale, a satisfied customer can be a potential recruit.

Here are some best practices you can use when recruiting new affiliates:

Try to attend all networking opportunities you can find. Especially those that are related to the service or product you are selling.

Set a daily goal for the number of people you will talk to about your product or about joining up. Stick to that goal as much as possible. Consistency is the key to reach more people at the shortest amount of time.

Keep in touch with repeat customers and those that provided you with positive feedback. Don't end your relationship after the sale. These people are potential recruits for your sales team.

Study your prospects. Even if they don't have the experience in this line of business they can become productive if you train and motivate them properly. What you'll need to consider first is the attitude of each prospect before recruiting network-marketing affiliates.

Recruit for your core team and for your contact group. The more driven people should be part of your core team, while those more casual sellers go to your contact group. What's the difference? The core team is your veteran or elite team, while the contact group is your training and proving ground.

Recruit people who share the same values as you. It is hard to have people in your team who aren't willing to do what you need them to. You can probably add them up but not as a member of your core team.

Don't open up your conversations with your pitch. A little bit of small talk goes a long way. After the pleasantries, segue into your recruitment pitch. Listen first before you make a move. Sometimes the opportunity to make the pitch will come from the prospect himself. Even if you know you're offering a solution to his problem, make sure you hear it out first to make them know that you genuinely want to help.

Follow through with your recruits always. Call them on the phone to make a better impression if that is your style, personally I like email though. In this age of quick messaging, taking time to make a phone call or send an email gives the impression that they are important to you.

Go out and do it. Recruiting network marketing affiliates requires action. The time for planning is wasted if no action is taken.

A final word of advice: Don't ever spam your network group. People are more informed nowadays and flooding them with unsolicited messages is a good way to lose contacts or even friendships. Make connections, build rapport, and pitch your product then recruit!

Overcoming MLM Prospects' Reluctance

You have probably read a lot about how sales is a numbers game and that you need to approach a lot of people to be a success. It's a statistically proven fact – more leads equals more sales, but that's not the complete picture. There are other factors to consider. It is also important to know how to overcome MLM prospect reluctance.

Reluctance from an MLM prospect can have several causes. The most common ones are wrong impressions about network marketing, over saturation of MLM marketing opportunities and prior bad experience with MLM.

Sometimes these objections are like high brick walls. The right approach will allow you to dismantle it brick by brick. The wrong approach will be like hitting your head against a solid wall.

These issues are relatively tough to address but there are a few good practices that can help you overcome the reluctance of a promising MLM prospect. Even if they do totally refuse the offer, at least you can learn some very valuable marketing lessons.

Here are a few suggestions that can help you overcome the reluctance of an MLM prospect:

Never open up your pitch with the words "MLM" or "Networking". Too many shady businesses and marketers have abused this term. It now has negative connotations to a lot of MLM prospects. Always open up with the benefits of the product or the income opportunity. Network marketing incentives are just a component of the distribution process.

Join forums and read all negative reviews of MLM products. You will encounter a version of these complaints often and it is good to familiarize yourself with them. You'll either encounter a similar complaint or have a prospect that will tell you about hearing the complaint from a friend.

Learn all you can about your product through and through. Don't just read the provided material, read about the technology or the service itself. You need to give the impression that you're an expert on what you're marketing. Also, having more knowledge of your product helps you to sound more natural when you bring it up during conversation.

Become an advocate of your product. You should be using the product yourself and be an example of its benefits. Walk the talk – if you say this product or service has helped you then show actual proof. Not just in earnings but also in the positive effect on your quality of life. Emphasize the benefits to your lifestyle, health, and finances.

Do not take "NO" for an answer permanently. A negative response to your offer is normal. Not everyone is in a situation where they will need you're offering. Always leave an opportunity for you to reconnect with the lead in the future

Being a good marketer means you should be sensitive to your lead's mood. Persistence pays off but only if you keep yourself credible and likeable to your contacts. Here are a few examples: not spamming your lead list, not being pushy during your conversations, or simply respecting a lead's current decision.

If you can't close a sale, ask for a referral from your MLM prospect. In certain situations you may be able to get a referral from a lead that has refused your offer. This is one of the benefits of having a genuine rapport with your lead. Even if you haven't sold them anything yet, they can point you in the right direction.

These recommendations will only work for you if you put them into practice. Don't be afraid to make mistakes as long as you will own up to them. Experience has always been the most effective teacher in any field of study.

5 Avoidable Home Business Mistakes

New home business owners can sometimes be very enthusiastic and start a new business unprepared. Some of the more common mistakes are listed here:

Poor Market Research

Going into a business without knowing the market is a guaranteed way to waste your time and resources. Proper market research will show you the potential of your business idea. You'll know if it's feasible or not.

Your research should be able to determine how many potential customers you have in your target market. Is there a demand for what you want to sell? Who are the best suppliers for the materials or ingredients I need for my products? Will customers be able to afford what I'm selling? These and other important questions need to be answered before you can even start on planning your home business.

Do the require research before you make a move. Even though your plans will likely change, having the information you need to make the right decision is crucial to your enterprise's survival.

Poor Time Management

Time is money. This concept should motivate you enough to practice efficient time management. It's not just avoiding wasted time. It also involves streamlining your operation to ensure that your production and work processes are as efficient as you can make them.

The advantage of being able to produce something quickly won't be much of a benefit to your business, if your products aren't delivered on time. Bottlenecks in production need to be dealt with or your business will never take off.

Make it a habit to limit possible distractions in your work area, organize tasks, and prioritize doing things that will likely save you time in the future.

Poor Promotion and Marketing

What is the best way to spread word about your product?

How can you sell it effectively to your customers?

You need to have a good answer for these questions if you want to sustain your business' growth. In an ideal situation, marketing activities should take up a lot of your time. Running online campaigns, generating leads, and building up traffic for your website are just a few of the marketing tasks that require your consistent effort.

Take advantage of automated marketing tools to sustain momentum. Try multiple marketing channels and stick to those that work.

Poor Spending Strategy

Spending and not saving and then not spending when there is an opportunity to grow the business – these are few of the most common mistakes would be entrepreneurs make when running their business.

There are of course situations where it's obvious that you need to spend. Repairs, growing the business, and increasing stocks, are all good examples of situations when you should be spending money. Renovating and redecorating the office, buying a new car for the business, or upgrading your computers should never be done without in depth cost analysis.

Separate personal and business funds. Pay yourself a salary instead of getting money directly from your business' funds.

Lack of Contingency Plans

When your business hits a rough spot, you need to have a backup plan ready. Drops in sales due to a new competitor, a weakened economy, or a natural disaster can severely affect your operations and income. A contingency plan will help you keep minimize downtime and keep your online business going.

A good entrepreneur will have a contingency plan and the necessary resources in place ready for any emergency. The typical expectation is that your business should be up 98% of the time.

More seasoned business owners will likely tell you how they made these same mistakes when they were just starting out. They'd probably say that knowing the pitfalls your business may encounter is a huge advantage. They would be right.

Top Earner MLM Tips

The Multi Level Marketing concept has become widespread in the past few decades. Its adoption accelerated when Internet use became commonplace. MLM relies heavily on marketing to people at the consumer level and the availability of cheap but effective online advertising helped immensely.

The Top Earner MLM personalities are usually part of the 1st batch of members or affiliates. Sometimes they're actually the founders of the network. Even if you're not part of the initial seed group, you can still earn a significant amount.

Getting in early is one key to being a top earner MLM, but it's not the only factor that helps increase earnings. Being part of the initial core group is a huge advantage but they do have a responsibility to get everything up and running. They are the ones who will grow the network in its early phase. Aggressive recruiting is a key activity especially if the network has just been established.

Always create opportunities to network. This will help a lot in getting more people in to your team. A few successful and top earner MLM personalities often hold seminars to help train and motivate the members of their network. These seminars also create recruitment and sales opportunities. More affiliates usually lead to more sales.

Speaking of affiliates, most of the top earner MLM lists people who have invested in training their down-line. In turn those down-line are expected to train the people they recruit. Providing encouragement, product knowledge and sales training help keep the momentum going.

You also have to vary your approach depending on the person you're selling to or recruiting. Not everyone will appreciate hard sell tactics and neither does soft sell work all the time. A little finesse goes a long way especially with prospects that have been previously disappointed by MLM products.

Consistency of course is a basic requirement. You need to stay in the game and keep growing your network to reap the benefits. Top earner MLM lists have marketers who have been with their company for a significant amount of time. Most of them will likely see it through the end.

For beginners it may feel that your network is building up too slowly. Don't get discouraged. It really takes time to get the ball rolling. When you have built you sales team, always make sure to train them well. Don't be afraid to trim out the non-performing members. It is natural to get a few duds from time to time.

Each approach to a prospect must be carefully fit to the particular product and consumer. Study your product well and the market you intend to sell to. If you plan to sell health products to a doctor, will you be able to sufficiently explain what you're selling to him?

Top Earners have other best practices that they've honed through experience. They sometimes sell books about their tactics and strategies. This is good information to have and can save you some problems. Just make sure that you are getting materials from a reputable Top Earner MLM personality.

Part 2: Succeeding Online

This section of the book covers how to build a serious online network marketing business. We are going to give you specific strategies and resources to use in growing your team and your business.

Finding MLM Resources Online

Most beginner network marketers learn the ropes from their mentors or find MLM resources online. It's usually the person who introduced you to network marketing who becomes your mentor. However, you can't rely on him or her all the time for lessons and guidance. You have to strike out on your own and find MLM lessons from other sources.

Experience maybe the best teacher but proper training and preparation ensures that you minimize wasted opportunities. Every lead is precious and deserves your full effort.

Here are some sources of useful information and insights online:

Blogs

There are very talented and experienced network marketers who share practical MLM lessons on their blogs. You may want to bookmark and study a few of them.

Try to send the blogger a message and ask if you can do a guest post.

Forums

Join discussions and share your knowledge. Share your website and ask for feedback on how to improve it.

Social Media

There are several very active network marketing personalities on Facebook. Their account acts as an extension of their website or blog.

You should to build up a good list of network marketing leaders. They usually provide information that you can apply immediately to your own efforts.

Read comments, especially complaints. Learn from the mistakes of others and formulate your own approach to the complainer's situation.

Search Engine

This may seem like a very obvious suggestion but learning how to effectively use search engines allows you to find MLM resources that you can use.

Learn how to filter and narrow down results using the various operators like (*) and (-).

MLM Company Website

Another recommendation that sounds pretty obvious but if you haven't gone through all the company's materials then you may be leaving something out.

MLM Review sites

There are a lot of sites online that discourage people from joining MLM campaigns. A lot of their warnings do make sense, however these are only applicable if the MLM Company you joined up with is bogus.

Expect to see the same arguments brought up by a few of your leads. Reading these write-ups will help you prepare your own reply if they are brought up.

Online Mentors

There are a lot of experienced marketers who offer their time to mentor novices. Keep in touch with them and ask for advice.

Be wary of pretenders of course. If they spend more time trying to sell you something rather than answering your questions then you should probably drop them and find another teacher.

Niche Authority Websites

These sites carry information that will help you explain how your products work. This is especially true for health products. Expand you vocabulary and understand how the product works.

Often times the marketing material provided by the MLM company gives you a pretty narrow perspective on their product.

The Internet contains an almost inexhaustible amount of information about different topics that you encounter on a daily basis. Find MLM resources and study them to ensure that you are well prepared to reel in a new lead.

Online MLM Business Software Tools You Need to Master

If you're planning to join or have signed up for an online MLM business, here are a couple of critical software tools you'll need to build it up:

Autoresponder

A mailing list is a critical component of any online marketing business. Whether you're doing MLM, affiliate or retail, a responsive mailing list can provide you with a steady stream of income.

An auto responder software or online service enables you to build up your list and broadcast your message to the list members. Mastering its intricacies will help you build your list much faster.

Building a list is no easy task. A genuinely interested subscriber is hard to come by. Even if you have plenty of traffic coming your way, it's no guarantee that one of them will opt-in. This is why you need to have an auto responder that has the features that help you reach out effectively to members and potential subscribers.

Keyword Analysis Tools

This tool gives you a summary of the most searched for topics on a specific search engine.

People go online to search for information on things that interest them or are relevant to their needs. These searches are tracked by whatever search engine they use and with the right tools you can gather useful information from these records.

You can narrow down which keywords and topics people are searching for often. You can then use those words and topics in your blog posts, videos and articles. This will help you get into the search results page for these keywords.

Google has a free to use keyword analysis tool that provides you with the global and local search activity for a specific keyword. It also shows you the result for other related terms. It's basically a gold mine of information for people who want to market to a specific niche.

There are also paid software packages that provide more extensive keyword information. These can be a good investment especially if you use blogs as your primary traffic capture method.

Blogging Platform

There are several competing platforms in the current online environment. Although, WordPress tends to be the more commonly used because of the sheer amount of themes and plug-ins available.

Ideally, you should have enough knowledge to manage and configure your own blog. Even though there are free platforms and templates available, you want to be able to customize your own site.

There's a huge benefit to customization. If you look at other marketer's sites online, you will notice that a lot of them look alike with the same basic layout and font. This is because they're using the template provided by either their hosting site or MLM Company. You need to stand out from the crowd to be noticed and knowing how to customize your site gives you this capability.

Video Presentation software

Videos have become indispensable in today's highly competitive online business environment. They allow you to relay your message to potential customers in a very detailed manner.

Video editing is a useful skill but production value isn't really as important as the content. Once you're done recording, you just need to polish it up a bit so you can prepare it for upload.

There is another class of video software tools that allow you to convert presentation files into video. You can also combine straight video with your presentation and convert it to a format that can be uploaded to video sharing sites. This can really help you produce more informative material in an easily accessible format.

Top 3 Sources of Targeted Traffic for Your Home Business

If you're a home business owner and you want your business to reap the benefits of being on the internet, you'll need to focus on attracting traffic to your website.

There are a lot of options when it comes to generating traffic, but here are the top 3 most popular ones:

Blogs

Some owners of traditional businesses tend to dismiss blogs altogether. They ignore it because they believe it is more important to focus on sales over building relationship with customers. They don't want to spend time and effort to get a blog to rank and they are usually unfamiliar with the intricacies of page optimization.

It's just so much easier to buy advertising space on existing popular websites. However, it can become a ridiculously expensive exercise even in the short term. Advertising should not only pay for itself, it should also help you crack new markets and build up a loyal customer base – exactly what a blog can do for your business.

A properly ranked blog can be considered a gold mine when it comes to getting new sales. A high ranking website with steady amount of targeted traffic is well worth the effort to build up.

Don't be afraid of the seemingly insurmountable leads of established websites on the internet. There are a multitude of keyword search combinations that you can dominate and profit from. With the importance being given to local search, you now have the opportunity to compete for and dominate the traffic in an area that is relevant to your business.

Social Media Page

The total number of Facebook users has already surpassed 1 billion. Twitter, Instagram and LinkedIn have user populations easily in the millions and these are only figures for the more popular sites. Niche social networking sites have their own following too.

As a business owner, it would be illogical to ignore these numbers, especially when access to them is virtually free. If you want more people to know about your business, then you have to have a presence here.

Social networking is here to stay. It has revolutionized how people use the internet in much the same way the World Wide Web did. You can even consider it as one of the important requirements when you're setting up a business.

YouTube

It's the 2nd largest search engine albeit it focuses only on the videos in its database. Still, it has a huge amount of video content that gets around 3 billion page views every day. With a bit of effort, you can host your own video and use that to funnel viewers to your blog or website.

The catch here is that you really have to create quality content to get people to view your video. Aside from creating valuable video content, you'll need to work on sharing and spreading word about your video.

Before you even consider the paid sources, you should be maximizing what traffic you can get from these sites. They offer a cost effective source of quality traffic for your website.

Targeted traffic for your small business shouldn't cost you an arm and a leg. The effort you put in to develop these traffic sources will pay for themselves in the long run.

Part 3: Social Media Marketing

Social media is by far one of the best places to start with online business. Not only because you probably already have a warm market, but also because it can be done for either free or very cheap. This section goes over how you can do this successfully starting as early as today.

List of Social Networks for Sharing Your Content

You know you can create great content, whether it's a compelling article, an extremely enjoyable short video, or maybe you've written music that you know a lot of people will like. You want to share your work to the world for whatever reason that is important to you. Oftentimes it's for experience, sometimes to get it monetized, but always for recognition. Your list of social networks will reflect what sites you should be on and will depend on the nature of the content you create.

You start with websites that host your content: video sharing sites, torrent networks, blogs, and sites for independent artists. Some social networking sites allow you to upload content directly. This is less than ideal since you might need to tweak the privacy settings to allow people to view your work. There is also a possibility that the site is blocked in certain locations. Your list of social networks should large enough to mitigate some of these concerns.

Making your work available online is only the first step. You'll need to do promotions that will help you showcase your work beyond your immediate contacts. It is now standard strategy to promote your work on multiple social networks. They may not by themselves guarantee your success but not being on them increases the likelihood of failure. Your web must also be wider to ensure you catch more opportunities to increase your exposure.

You will need to build up your following on these sites to make your promotion more effective. I've listed down two sets of social networking sites. The top 5 are the most popular ones and you need to be on these sites. The second list of social networks features those that have a respectable follower base. They're like the backup singers to your front act. Promotions there are still worth your while.

My Top 5

Facebook – Since it has the most number of users on the planet, it's a no-brainer that you have to promote yourself here. It can become expensive especially now that they charge for promoting posts, but if you have a respectable amount of followers here, you can opt to promote only to them.

Twitter – This is another very popular site and has one of the fastest response times. You can pay them to promote your post to a large section of their users but you can also contact accounts with huge followings to have your post tweeted to their followers. The cost will be higher if you go to accounts that have a lot of followers. You can also build your own follower base but that takes time plus you need to be either already popular or have a very interesting and compelling feed.

Instagram – This is the most popular photo sharing application on mobile phones that makes it perfect for sharing visual content. You can also share pictures of your work or ask existing accounts to share it. Again numbers matter here, the more followers the more effective your

Google+ – this is has gotten a lot of flak for coming in late to the social networking game. Still, Google is the largest search engine online and their efforts in any field are worth taking note of. The fact that they are pushing for making recommendations via Google+ matter to search keeps their site relevant.

Pinterest – This is another site that's focused on picture sharing. A neat thing about Pinterest, aside from their phenomenal growth, is the ability to add URLs into the post. This is very useful when you want to redirect users to your main site. For video content, you can post a screen shot of the video and then redirect people to where it's hosted.

My Secondary List

Tumblr – It has a large user base but it is considered more of a content generation site than a full pledged social network. Its existing social features are enough to help you with sharing content.

Linkedin – This is very useful for business to business networking. If your content's topic is more related to business and industry, then this network should be at the top of your list of social networks.

MySpace – It was once king of the social networking realm, it has been knocked off that position by Facebook and has since re-tooled itself. It's now a popular site for artists and performers, especially independent ones. This is a great site to be on if your promoting music content.

Tagged, Hi5 and Bebo- These sites have occupied a small but very active niche. They are considered as the social networking sites for meeting new people as opposed to Facebook that mainly features existing friends. What's neat is some of these sites use Facebook's login to connect that makes them very useful tools for building up your existing Facebook profiles.

Deviant Art – It was considered the 13th largest social network last July 2011. The site is focused on graphical content whether for applications or print. Its community is quite active and the best content posted here is shared on other sites as well.

There are several other niche social networking sites and communities you can add to your list. You will probably end up with your own list of social networks. What's important is establishing your presence on the most popular sites AND making sure you are also present on the sites that are important to your subject matter.

Effective Social Network Page Management for Home Business

A smart business owner should always try to maximize the use of resources. This not only includes those that he's paid for, but also those tools that are available to use for free.

One of the most powerful free resources are Social Networking Sites. They allow you to interact with your customers, show off your brand or business, and potentially attract more customers.

Between two competing businesses that offer the same level of quality, customer service and pricing, the one with a well-managed social media presence has the definite advantage. We are rapidly approaching an era where not having an effective social media presence can be a crippling disadvantage. For areas with widespread internet use, we might have already passed the threshold.

Small business owners may not have enough time or manpower to manage a social media profile page. So they have to really make sure that whatever time they spend is used for the best effect.

Here are a couple of suggestions on how to make effective use of Social Media resources:

Choose the network that is popular with your customers.

Don't waste your time managing multiple social media profiles when only one profile generates useful interactions. There is no sense being on Twitter if most of your users interact with you on Facebook. The time spent updating other sites could be used more productively in crafting quality posts on your customer's preferred sites.

This doesn't mean that you shouldn't maintain a presence on the popular sites, but you can definitely use them to redirect people to your more active Social Networking page.

Separate your Brand's voice from your Personal one.

Setup a separate account for your business. Avoid posting anything of a personal nature if you're using your brand's name. It would look unprofessional if you posted something about your personal life under the name of your online store. However, you can post personal stuff from time to time if you're using your own profile to post, and people know you're part of the business.

Maintain a consistent presence.

Check your social media page regularly. Try to allot at least an hour daily to interact with your customer's posts. Even a simple "like" or "re-tweet" can have a positive effect. Post something interesting on a daily basis. It can be an article you like from a relevant site or a photo that's related to the business. Marketing posts are fine as long as they don't spam your business page.

Post Interesting and Relevant links, articles or pictures.

If you're business sells a particular product, post an article that's related to it. For example, if your business sells photography equipment then your customers will likely appreciate a post on photography techniques.

There is a huge amount of free to share information online; posting articles that interest your customer isn't that hard. You can also share humorous content or current events, but try to make sure this won't turn off your followers or start an argument on your page.

The primary goal of posting relevant content is to encourage engagement and create a positive impression of your business or brand. If your post will not result in either, then it's better not to post anything at all. You can probably get away with posting simple greetings if you don't have any good content for posting yet.

Frequency of Posts depends on the site you're using.

One of the most common questions about posts is about frequency. How often should you update? The answer actually varies depending on the social network you're on. Obviously, spamming and flooding are frowned upon, but not posting enough in a day will likely bury your post on your follower's feeds.

A good rule of thumb would be around 5- 6 times spread across 24 hours for Twitter and once a day for Facebook – this applies to regular content. If there are any relevant breaking news then try to post as soon as you have all the important information or you can acknowledge the event and tell your followers you'll update them once you have all the info.

Since your Facebook page is likely going to be your most active page, make sure your customers allow your posts to be shown on their feeds. Facebook has been tweaking the visibility of posts quite often as part of their monetization strategy. Try to stay on top of these changes so that you can take the necessary actions to make sure your page remains visible to your loyal followers.

For Twitter users, your posting strategy and frequency will vary significantly. Some users like to converse over Twitter, others use it more for broadcasting. Both approaches will vary the number of Tweets that are posted per day, but you should still avoid flooding your followers' feed. A short burst of conversational tweets is tolerable. If longer conversations are needed then you should move it to a chat room, conference or Google hang out.

Do not oversell your business on your page (or any other page for that matter).

A well run, useful and relevant business page will sell your brand by itself. Avoid spamming your own page with marketing posts. Stick to a daily schedule of updates unless you're running a promo.

Even then try to limit the posts so that it doesn't flood your follower's feed.

Promos are welcome BUT...

As with other types of posts, try not to flood your followers' feeds. Remember the main reason you're running a promotion is to attract more customers or more fans. Spamming, no matter how amazing the offer, will be looked upon negatively. You don't want to risk mass unlikes and unfollows. If you're running a contest, a daily update is enough to build excitement over who is winning.

Discuss important messages privately.

Take sensitive discussions into private messaging. A good example is a customer who brings a personal issue. You really don't want your customers to get the wrong impression before you resolve it. If it's really important, moving it to email or scheduling a call may be a more effective way to reach a resolution.

Never, Ever, Ever Argue on your Business Page.

I cannot stress how important this is. The same goes for having a condescending attitude on your posts. The fallout alone from this type of fiasco can be fatal to your online reputation. It can reach a point where you'll need professional help to fix your online credibility. Take the discussion into a private channel, offer to do a private chat, and, if you can verify that it's a questionable profile, report the user to the site's admin or block it outright.

One more thing.

Always clean up your page. Some users follow groups so they can spam them with marketing offers. Be firm about this. Don't be afraid (or be too lazy) to remove them from your group. The loss of one spammy follower will help you maintain a clean, useful feed and keep your real followers happy.

Strategies for MLM Online Marketing on Twitter

Twitter is a powerful news dissemination tool. A staggering potential for generating sales is present. With the proper approach, you can use it for MLM online marketing.

The key is to establish credibility and then work your niche. Cast your net far and wide to get an active set of followers then market to them. It's not something that you can accomplish in just a few months. You need to let your account and relationship with your followers mature.

One thing you need to remember about social media sites like Twitter and Facebook is that it only takes a few seconds for a user to block you. A user, can on a whim, block you if he thinks you're just pitching products at him. You need to establish a connection first.

And it's not just about the numbers. Some mistakenly believe that you can get a lot of good sales just by having a lot of followers. Same for those who try to saturate their feed with sales offers.

You won't accomplish anything by giving the impression you're a bot. Users prefer to listen to real people, like you do. Don't doom your MLM online marketing efforts by being insensitive to your followers.

Getting Started:

- Flesh out your profile info and theme. Use an eye-catching background picture that features your site's theme.

- Establish a follower base. Follow every Active Twitter user you know and discretely ask for them to follow you back. It's great if you start with close friends or acquaintances since they will likely converse with you.

- Make sure your twitter profile link is present on all your online contact info

- Make it easier for Twitter users to comment on your site. Enable log-ins via Twitter.

Growing your Follower base:

- Join discussions and use trending topic hash tags

- Follow profiles that are interested in the same topics as you. Check their biographies.

- Reply to comments by established profiles. Try to establish dialog. Post interesting, witty and relevant replies.

- Utilize sponsored posts

- Run a contest to get new followers. For example: rewards for being the 1,000th follower.

Establishing Your Reputation:

- Consistently engage your followers. Show you care about them. Be gracious and tactful all the time.

- Be generous with retweets.

- Run contest to give free samples of a new product.

- Use your twitter profile for commenting on posts in reputable websites.

- Never post a link that goes directly to a capture page, unless you give notice that it is one.

- Share relevant photos.

- Space your Tweets. Don't Flood people's feeds. If you need to reply immediately ask a user to follow you so you can direct message them.

Working on your Niche:

- Post links to resources related to your niche.

- Post a link to every new post you put on your blog, Facebook, Instagram or Pinterest

- When posting an offer, try not to be too pushy about it. Your follower's Feed is like their living room; they can kick out unwanted guests anytime.

Your Twitter profile should be interesting, relevant and useful to your followers. They won't mind a marketing post now and then if they feel you're being very tactful about it. Effective MLM online marketing on Twitter requires that you make your followers feel like they're following a human being and not a hard-nosed salesman.

How to get Facebook Fans on a Tight Budget

A few years back, we were handed the task of building up our Facebook fans. It was our first time to do this sort of task and we weren't yet familiar with the strategies used to funnel fans to a Facebook page. We had to do some research and test our strategies through trial and error.

We set our initial target to 1,000 fans and we wanted these to be all active. We wanted to build a community of fans on our Facebook page. We knew that being able to engage customers through social networking would benefit us a lot. It also didn't hurt to have a group of people who could spread word about us. At this time, we were familiar with how powerful social networking was and how it could significantly improve our sales volume.

These were the steps we tried out:

-        Sent invites to members of our mailing list. We also put in the URL for our page on the signature.

-        We added a Facebook badge to our website. This seemed to get more people joining up.

-        We asked a few of our Twitter contacts to share the link to our page. Our Twitter profile didn't have that many active fans so I asked a favor from a few of our more loyal followers.

- We put the link to our page on our menu, flyers and front door.

- We regularly posted interesting and funny posts that we asked our existing fans to share or discuss. Facebook automatically mentions your post on a user's feed if they "like" it or comment on it.

- It took us about 2 months to get to 400 followers. We then ran a "most likes" photo contest and had some actual prizes for the winner. It was a gift certificate that we sent through email and that you could print out. This got a lot of attention and we quickly had people signing up. We ran it for about a month and had weekly winners. On hindsight, we thought that it wouldn't have been that successful if not for the initial 400+ followers.

It took around 7 months to get to 1,000 followers. We did get a number of people leaving the page after a few customers posted complaints. I took care of that promptly and made sure it didn't spill out too much on our main feed. It's very important to isolate customer complaints and deal with them in private. We had it all sorted out eventually using private messaging and emails.

How to get Facebook fans if we had a bigger budget? We would have used solo ads to get more fans. A bigger promotion and a contest with a bigger prize would have worked too. The click to pay ads in Facebook would've also been something we would consider.

Genuine engagement and timely replies really help keep the fans loyal to your business. I believe this was the most important lesson

I've learned from the campaign. I've written these instructions without specifying what type of business we have because the steps are usable by any type of business.

Part 4: Email Marketing

Email marketing is one of the most effective means of online marketing you can do. Much of what we have already talked about with social media will apply here too. However, I wanted to explore a couple of facets of email marketing specifically so you understand the importance of them and how to use this channel effectively.

HTML Email Newsletters: What You Need To Know

What is an HTML Email Newsletter?

An Email Newsletter is a type of email that is periodically sent to a list of subscribers. These are often sent to mailing lists and users who have opt in to receive it. It typically contains information about new products, promotions, discoveries, etc.

Emails were initially only in text only format in the early days before widespread adoption. Once web based email services like Hotmail, Rocketmail and Yahoo mail caught on, the creators of these services wanted to provide users with the basic word processing features found on popular email clients. Enabling HTML tags was the first step.

Eventually, as the popularity of web based email exploded, links, images and even CSS formatting were added. As internet connections increased in speed and capacity, it became possible for web based email clients to implement the full range of features offered by traditional email clients like Lotus & Outlook. The tables have actually turned for these email client providers as they now offer web based versions of their software.

HTML Email Newsletter Advantages

It's graphically oriented; you can use different fonts and colored backgrounds. A wide selection of html tags used for presentation can be used.

Using colors and pictures on your email newsletter increases the amount of information that can be conveyed to the reader.

You can track if the receiver has opened the mail. This is an important feature for marketers.

You can launch interactive features within the email itself. A clickable link can be placed on the email that can funnel users to a new page (usually a product page)

A lot of available tools for creating an html email newsletter are available. Choose one that matches your level of proficiency.

Disadvantages

You'll need some knowledge of HTML coding, although templates and wizards are available now. Email auto response providers like Aweber and Mailchimp have a good selection of themes and templates. Gmail and Yahoo mail do allow you to create basic HTML emails but they don't have newsletter functions.

An HTML Email Newsletter may take longer to load than text based email but this can be sped up by good design.

Some graphical and interactive elements can be blocked by email clients. Hackers and phishing scam artists who hid malicious links in emails brought on this precaution.

Email design can vary if opened on different browsers or devices, sometimes rendering the email unreadable. Again good design and preparation can mitigate this issue.

Some email clients will only display the text version of an email. This is typically a security setting to limit phishing scams and bad redirects.

Lastly, a lot of tools are available for creating an html email newsletter. Not all of these tools will display standard output on various email platforms. A bevy of options almost always creates fragmentation of the platform. There are efforts to address this through the establishment of industry standards.

Best Practices

Always use text for the main message. If you put your message up as a graphic, you risk the possibility of the customer not seeing it if graphics display is off by default or if they are using a text only email client.

Do not attach files to your newsletters. Use file hosting and sharing services instead. Attachments bog down loading of the message. You can also offer to send attachments to interested subscribers. This is an excellent way to interact with them.

Design your html email newsletter to be easily readable no matter what device or client is in use. Send your draft to yourself and open it on different devices and email clients. Fine tune your design to make sure everything looks good on the most commonly used platforms.

The tracking option is very useful for measuring the effectiveness of your campaign. Auto response services and software allows you to generate reports and check the effectiveness of your newsletter.

Try to add only the bare minimum pictures needed. Don't overload the newsletter with photos. Entice people to the visit your website instead by using a combination of good copywriting and elegant newsletter design.

HTML email newsletters are great for digests and summaries of updates on your website. It is also great for showcasing new products or promotions. It is simply a better way to present your message and provide your subscribers with more information.

Tips for Writing an Effective Email Subject Line

The subject line is a critical component of your newsletter and marketing email. It acts much like a newspaper headline; its job is to get your attention and tell something about the top news for the day. A great subject line will get a person interested enough to want to open the email you sent.

Short and sweet is the perfect phrase to sum up what makes a great headline. Here are some of its characteristics:

-        Gives an idea of the content

-        Instills a sense of urgency

-        Clear and Concise

-        Appeals to subscriber's interests

-        Elicits curiosity

There are a ton of best practices being touted by online experts. Some of these you need to do and cannot afford to skip. Others are more situational and will require a bit of trial and error on your part.

Here are some tips for writing an effective Email Subject Line:

Keep within the subject line's character limit. You'll want to make sure you get the most impact out of the space provided. A subject like with too many words will likely be cut and won't look neat. The total number of visible characters varies depending on the user's settings on his email program, his screen resolution, and what devices he uses it on.

Here are the counts for the most commonly used email clients:

-        Yahoo Mail (new version) – 46 characters

-        Gmail – 70 characters

-        IPhone – 41 characters portrait mode, 64 characters landscape mode.

Avoid Spam Filters. There are two things that are commonly used as triggers for spam filters: an email address from a domain name with a bad reputation; and specific keywords on the subject line. You have direct control over both. When it comes to the subject line, avoid using words that everyone will likely filter. Words like "Viagra" are a good example. Check your spam mail folder to see other examples of words you should avoid.

Tone and Choice of words should fit your subscribers. You might be tempted to use some jargon in your subject line to make it sound authoritative, or you might go in the opposite direction and use some colloquial terms. If you want to make sure your email isn't ignored, you need to match the vocabulary of your mailing list. Keep in mind the composition of the audience you're sending the email to.

Copy best practices. Don't cut and paste. Copy or better yet, get inspiration from marketers who have been successful in the email marketing field. You'll learn a lot just by reading through the title of the emails you received from them. Save subject lines that worked well for you, especially ones that you've read and made you open a particular email

Here are some other tips you can try:

-       Use a question as your subject line. These can be excellent calls to action.

- WIFM or what's in it for me. Emphasize potential value of email

- Avoid these words: Free, Help, Discount

- Familiarity helps. Make use of headlines referencing local topics, places, or people.

- Share not Sell. A customer follows your list because they find value in your product. Don't use it to push sales all the time or you risk getting filtered out.

- Add your Brand to the Subject line. Do this only if your brand has established a reputation.

Remember; a good headline should make someone take notice of your email; an effective email subject line makes one want to read the whole email.

Improve Your Online Earnings Using Solo Ads

What are Solo Ads?

Solo Ads are a service that you can purchase from an owner of a mailing list. He will send an email on your behalf with an offer and link to your chosen page. Cost is usually based on the number of guaranteed clicks or subscribers on the list. It can become quite expensive to do Solo Ads so its best used when you have an effective landing page and compelling product.

Since solo ads are shared through an active mailing list, there is a higher chance that you can get actual subscribers from the same list. It's all up to you to make sure you can entice them to sign up to your own list.

Solo Ads are great when you're just starting out with your campaign or building your own mailing list. You really need guaranteed traffic to give your campaign the exposure it needs and solo ads can give you that critical push.

Here's a guide and list of tips on how to take advantage of solo ads:

- Find a solo ads provider. Send him the target URL and ad copy you want to be sent out to his list.

- There are established Solo Ads providers available online and there are also sites where you can see a list of providers.

- Choose the provider whose list is composed of people who are in your target niche. You will get a better response rate this way compared to using lists that cover wide topics.

- The target URL sends people to your own website or sales page where they can join your mailing list or buy a product.

- You'll need to create an incentive for users to sign up to your own list. This can be anything from a free report, video or product promos.

- You can get some quick sales from people who sign up by offering them a special "one time" offer that they can only purchase after they sign up.

- Try to vary your offers each time you send a new ad. You can also use other providers to see which has a more responsive list.

- It is important to remember that people sign up to your list because they will have the impression that you have something unique to offer. Try to offer special deals or share great content to keep your list engaged.

Running Solo ads is one of the best marketing methods I've used. I was able to build a decent list of people from my target niche. Since my primary niche is social media marketing, I usually get a significant number of list members interested in my social media campaign support services.

Always remember: once you've built a sizable list you should continue to nurture and grow it with new solo ads campaigns. Try to limit the amount of times you post in a week. You don't want to send to emails too often and end up getting tagged as spam. Don't waste the money you've invested to build your list by giving them reasons to leave it.

Part 5: Putting It All Together

Now that you have an understanding of all the different resources and tools available, its time to put it all together. This chapter will outline a step-by-step plan you can use to grow your network marketing business using the internet.

It will reference lots of the tools and resources already mentioned in previous parts of the book. By the end of it, you will have a path that you can follow to get started with your online business.

At the end of the day, growing a network marketing business is about being a leader. However there are many paths to leadership and no one way will be the same. This portion of the book will lay out a general path for you to follow but you should always be adapting your business to your own personal strengths and style of business.

Specific details will not be discussed, such as how to effectively use social media or how to write email headlines, as those have already been covered earlier in the book.

Your Network Marketing Online Business Plan

The business plan we are going to provide here is going to be centered around one thing: your personal network of contacts. Network marketing, by its very name, relies on this.

Everything you do online should have a single end goal: to add people to your network of contacts that are likely to buy from you or join your opportunity.

Your network of contacts is what allows you to grow your business and increase your revenues. Once you have a large enough network, you can reach out to them any time you want, whether it be with a new product or service or a new business opportunity.

As you have learned, there are many places you can grow your contact list:

- By getting more followers, friends and fans on Facebook, Twitter, LinkedIn and other social networks
- By increasing the viewership of your YouTube channel
- By publishing an email newsletter and increasing your readership
- By adding more loyal readers of your blog and getting them on your email list

As you build each of these channels up, you will have more and more reach. The more reach you have online, the bigger your network of contacts becomes. Eventually it will grow all by itself as people share your social profiles, posts, videos, articles and other content.

The easiest way to get started with all of this is to setup Facebook page for yourself. Note that this is NOT a personal profile. This is a dedicated page for you.

Many people in this industry will tell you the first thing you need to do is setup a personal blog. What I have found though is that most people get bogged down in all the technical knowledge it takes to setup a blog. They get frustrated, get lost or just plain quit before they have even started.

A great alternative to this is a Facebook page. I like pages for lots of reasons:

- They are completely free to setup
- They are accessible to everyone
- Most people already understand and are on Facebook anyway
- Facebook has lots of traffic that you can tap into right away

Setting up a Facebook page is a relatively straight forward process. Just sign into Facebook, go to the pages sections and click "Create A Page".

As you set up your page, or any of your social profiles, be sure to make it look real. You want a picture of you for the main profile image, add other images of your life and fill out the about sections in your own voice.

The internet is impersonal because of its electronic nature. Your objective when designing any of your social profiles, blogs or websites is to make them as personal as possible.

Once you have your Facebook page up and running, it's a good idea to go ahead and setup a Twitter profile, a LinkedIn profile, a Google+ profile and a YouTube channel. This will cover 95% of all social media.

Optionally you can setup profiles on other social networks and videos sites but these are the major ones and really all you need.

Once you have your social profiles setup, you will need to start the actually networking process. There are a few components to this:

- Creating and sharing your own content
- Sharing and re-sharing other people's content
- Engaging people in public conversation
- Engaging people in private conversation
- Adding people to your network of contacts

The whole idea is to create lots of conversation and content sharing that all revolves around you and your various social profiles. This allows people to get to know, you build trust with you and ultimately a relationship with you.

The more public of a figure you are online, the more influence you will have and the more your network marketing business will grow.

Lets breakdown each of these elements so you understand how to grow your online presence.

1.   Creating and sharing your own content – This is the most time intensive element. Creating blog posts, YouTube videos, articles and other content pieces takes time and effort but is well worth the rewards. You just have to be sure that you share everything you create so you get payoff for your efforts.

2.   Sharing and re-sharing other people's content – This is simply posting a link, retweeting or reblogging content someone else has created. It shows you are a party of the online community and willing to endorse quality work done by other people. It is also an easy way to start a conversation since you don't have to create any content of your own.

3.   Engaging people in public conversation – Public conversations over Twitter, comments on your Facebook page, replies in social media groups and other public conversations are

extremely powerful. Every post you make is public so it allows you to directly engage one or a few people, but you also indirectly engage tens or hundreds of other people that are monitoring the conversation.

4.   Engaging people in private conversation – Private conversation has been and always will be the most intimate of communication methods. They are time consuming but it is the one-way humans bond directly with each other. You won't have time to engage everyone privately but be sure to reply to everyone that messages you if at all possible.

5.   Adding people to your network of contacts – This is the end goal of all of your social networking and content sharing. The more you participate in the social media universe, the more people will add you. You can also add other people you think are good connections to have.

After you have established yourself on the major social networks, you should strongly consider building yourself a personal blog. A personal blog is the ultimate internet business asset because it is dedicated to you.

Its your blog and you have full control over it. This means you can scale up your business promotions beyond the limits of what most social networks will tolerate.

This is also where you can really build a powerful email newsletter subscriber list. Having a blog that feeds your email list on a daily basis is the single most powerful thing you can have as you build your online business.

You should be aware that this is where it is going to take a bit of time to understand the more technical side of the internet. Some people make a fulltime living just from having a strong social network presence. But if you really want to be able to grow and scale your online business properly, you will need a blog and email list.

The basic idea is that you drive as much traffic as possible to your blog. One of the ways you can do this is through social media as we have already mentioned. All you need to do is write a blog post or shoot a video blog and share that around your social networks.

Your social media following will see you sharing this content and click on the link. The link will take them to your blog.

Now that they are on your blog you have full control over their internet browsing experience. There are no Facebook or Twitter updates or new YouTube videos being posted to distract them.

They will look over your content and if it is good enough, they will browse around your blog and some of them will sign up for your email newsletter.

The point is that they are consuming only information you provide them with. Of course you should give them a good experience by providing quality content but you should also be encouraging them to sign up for your email newsletter, to check out recommended products and services or to join your business opportunity.

One point to remember as you consider starting your own blog: your blog will not have any traffic when it is first launched. This is the main reason I recommend building your social networking presence first.

If you already have a social network presence and a decent following, you will have blog traffic you can start sending right away. If you launch your blog first, but don't have any traffic, you are going to spend a lot of time going through the technical learning curve only to realize you have no visitors once your blog is live.

Its much easier and much more rewarding to build your social media traffic first and then launch your blog.

However when the time does come for you to build your personal blog, you will need to acquire the following:

- A domain name
- A hosting account
- Blogging software to install

Once you have these you will be ready. You can grab a domain name over at Godaddy.com. For hosting there are lots of options so you will need to do a bit of research. As for the blogging software, I highly recommend using Wordpress.

Wordpress is free and is the internet standard when it comes to blogging platforms. Many hosting companies provide scripts that will install if for you automatically.

One final tip: Getting traffic is the number one issue for 99% of people that try to start an internet business. There are plenty of products, services and business opportunities, but traffic is the biggest challenge when you first get started.

The social networking plan you have just been provided with is your solution to getting traffic for these reasons:

- Its free to start
- The social networks already have traffic you can tap into
- It requires minimal technical skills
- It is very high quality traffic due to the personal connection
- Most people already have social media accounts
- Anyone can do it if they really want to

Hundreds of millions of dollars have been made using social media strategies like this. Yes it does take some time and effort but everything in business does. The only question left, is are you going to utilize the knowledge you now have to build your own online network marketing business?

Bonus Chapters

These bonus chapters contain a few closing thoughts that every home business entrepreneur should consider. As you master online network marketing, they will help you continue to maintain the momentum necessary to succeed in your business and to take your life to the next level.

Sustaining Enthusiasm For Your Online Business

If you're in the habit of starting things but have a poor record of finishing them, you're not alone. A lot of people are great at starting something new. However, there's a tendency for them to lose enthusiasm and focus if some time passes without seeing any results.

A lot of the most successful entrepreneurs have the same "problem", but instead of treating it as a weakness, they use it to their advantage. They push themselves when their enthusiasm is at the highest point and take steps to sustain it. Not only do they focus on setting their business up, but they have a clear end goal in mind.

Whenever a great idea forms in our mind and takes hold of us, our focus and energy levels spike up. Our enthusiasm builds up and we want to get everything up and running. We want to see if our idea would work and we want to see the results as soon as possible.

If the idea doesn't require a lot of effort to implement, then it won't need much time to learn if it can work. Maybe you want to tweak your email campaign, design a new ad, or maybe offer your products in a new marketplace. These small tasks are easily completed and yield immediate results.

Bigger projects, like setting up a new business, takes more time and effort before you can start reaping rewards. This is where a lot of would-be entrepreneurs fail. Their drive to succeed tapers off because of the time it takes to reach their goals. It's sad to see a lot of failed start-ups and home businesses just because the owner suddenly lost interest.

Here are a few tips on how to consistently finish what you set out to do:

- Ask for help. Get someone to help you out by tracking your progress. A coach or a mentor can do this for you, but if you just want help you stay in focus, you can ask a friend or colleague to check on you from time to time. You and your buddy can review a list of what you've accomplished towards your goal. A buddy can help you stay focused and on track.

- Work on your project first at the start of your day. Make it your first priority and work on it at the most productive time of the day for you. Do as much as you can while you can maintain your focus.

- List down what you've accomplished on a daily basis. It's always heartening to know how much progress you've made. You can use applications that are designed for this type of activity or go the old fashioned way and write it down in a notebook. Whatever medium you use, make it a habit to write and review. Sometimes we just need to see how much progress we've made to keep our enthusiasm up.

- Clearly visualize your end game. What do you want to achieve? What are your non-negotiables? What benefits do you expect? If you don't have a clear goal, then it'll be pretty hard for you to measure progress and success. This lack of personalized vision is common with a lot of would be online entrepreneurs. Either jumping on a bandwagon, or haven't concretized their own goals and had someone dictate what it's supposed to be for them.

Not everyone has the opportunity to launch an online business. Those who have the resources and skills can ensure their enterprise succeeds by focusing on the present while keeping the future in mind.

Thinking of Putting your Home Business on Auto-Pilot?

Is it possible to put your Home Business on auto-pilot?

We'll define "on auto-pilot" as having the business fully independent and requires no direct input from the owner to keep operating. It should continue to earn and ideally grow with minimum intervention.

In specific circumstances, a business can run by itself, but it probably isn't something you can do in the long term. Limited automation maybe your best bet.

Is your business suited for automation?

Some businesses are easier to put on auto-pilot. It depends a lot on how much of the operation can be automated. A one man business typically can't operate without the business owner.

A business like consulting or remote support won't be able to function without the people who provide the services. If that person is you then you won't be able to leave it.

So called "passive income" online businesses can operate with minimum supervision, but won't grow without anyone taking care of business development. Businesses like affiliate marketing and network marketing rely heavily on quality advertising and promotion. However, these businesses can be left to run on their own if you have the right tools and well trained staff.

Here are some tools and strategies that will help you put your home business on auto-pilot:

- Applications that allow you to schedule posting to social media sites like Facebook and Twitter.

- Auto responder software that sends scheduled emails, and also sends canned replies if someone replies

- An automated marketing system that does a lot of the work for you.

- Hire a team of remote support staff and train them. You'll need to get an efficient project manager if you want to make sure that work is getting done.

- Get an assistant who is capable of running it for you. This might be the same person who handles part of your day to day operations.

- Automated payment and delivery system. Some affiliate marketers and drop sellers don't have inventory. They only maintain and promote a portal that relays purchases to the actual product vendor.

- Consolidated real time reporting tools. You need this to know how your business is performing on a day to day basis. It should provide you with a detailed summary of the current state of your operations at a glance. You shouldn't need to read through several reports just to know that.

How will you know that your business is ready for a less hands-on approach from you?

If you have the systems, personnel and tools you need in place, then step back from operations for a day or two and see how much work piles up. Check what sorts of tasks are left that need direct input from you. Determine if they can be delegated to your staff especially those that are urgent. If you're left with only a half an hour or so of tasks that you need to do, you're very likely on your way to having your business run by itself.

Is your Home Business truly on Auto-Pilot?

In the strictest sense, it is not. Your business needs your input to grow. It needs a direction, but then, if you set up the systems properly, you don't need to be the one doing the heavy lifting and the grunt work. You're only input will probably be approving the budget, reading reports, and figuring out the quarter's marketing plan

A lot of entrepreneurs typically aim for this sort of scenario. Reaping the rewards of their business while hardly moving a finger. It is possible to build one but it takes time before an organization that can function this way. Still, the thrust for more automation and proper delegation in any business provides its own rewards. It may not be running by itself, but it'll surely be running more efficiently.

Epilogue

I truly hope you have enjoyed reading this and found great value in it. Everything shared here has brought me a lot of success. I truly hope you can apply it just as effectively to your business so that you can have the success you deserve.

Don't forget to stop by my personal blog at **EricWelke.com** and join the free newsletter. I send out content on a regular basis that you will find useful. It will help you continue to be successful as you build your business.

Also be sure to go to **http://ericwelke.com/readerbonus** to download the secret bonus exclusively for readers.

Thanks for reading!

We Want Your Feedback on This Book!

Our main purpose is to make sure that our readers get value from the books we publish and that they have a good experience with all of our products. We are always working to improve our books and other products with every revision and update.

Every piece of feedback makes a difference in this process. And we would appreciate yours as well - whether it is good or bad.

Please take one minute to let us know what you thought by following this link:

http://ericwelke.com/bookfeedback

4092104R00062

Printed in Great Britain
by Amazon.co.uk, Ltd.,
Marston Gate.